Ayuvaddana Kumaraya

©2015 All Rights Reserved

ISBN: 978-955-687-037-4

Computer Typesetting by

Mahamevnawa Buddhist Monastery, Toronto
Markham, Ontario, Canada L6C 1P2
Telephone: 905-927-7117
www.mahamevnawa.ca

Published by

Mahamegha Publishers
Waduwawa, Yatigaloluwa, Polgahawela, Sri Lanka.
Telephone: +94 37 2053300 | 77 3216685
www.mahameghapublishers.com
mahameghapublishers@gmail.com

Ayuvaddana Kumaraya

With the guidance and direction of
Most Venerable Kiribathgoda Gnānānanda Thera

Artwork by Sumathipāla & Jothipāla

A Mahamegha Publication

Auwaddana Kumaraya

My dear children, every good thing that we have received in this life is a result of merits. The person who collects merits is saved from great disasters, rescued from great dangers and acquires great success in life. This story is about a young boy who was saved from a dangerous threat and achieved a good life by collecting merits.

During the time of the Buddha, there was a city called 'Dheegalanghika' in India. Two Brahmin men from this city ordained as Ascetics and lead an austere way of life for forty eight years. Oneday, one Ascetic thought, "this Brahmin ancestry of mine is very noble in the world. It is an admirable lineage. If I continue this Ascetic life, I will not be able to help continue my family line. Therefore, I must contribute a child to this lineage."

Then he went to his family and said "Dear Brahmins, I led an ascetic life for forty eight years. I have gained many great merits. Now, I would like to contribute a child to foster the continuation of this great Brahmin lineage. If someone is willing to give

me a hundred cows, a hundred coins of gold and a maiden I would transfer to him all the merits I have gained by leading the ascetic life."

The fellow Brahmins agreed to this idea and gave him what he asked. He married a young maiden and started a new life. After a while a son was born to this new family. The other Brahmin who had ordained as an Ascetic came to see his old friend and his family. The Brahmin was very happy, and spoke to his wife saying,

"My dear, my old friend is here, we will visit him and take our child too to show him."

Afterwards, the Brahmin family went to see the Ascetic. Having gone, the Brahmin handed his child over to his wife and worshipped the Ascetic. Then the wife handed the child over to the Brahmin and also worshipped the Ascetic. "May you live long!" the Ascetic blessed both of them.

Next the Brahmin parents made their son worship the Ascetic. But the Ascetic did not bless him; he

remained silent. The Brahmin was puzzled and asked the Ascetic about it.

"When my wife and I worshipped you, you blessed wishing us a long life. But when our son worshipped you, you remained silent, you did not bless him with a long life. Is there any particular reason for that?"

"Yes, my friend, there seems to be a problem with your son's life. He does not have a long lifespan."

"What does that mean… how many years does he have to live?" asked the much worried Brahmin.

"Not years my friend, from what I see, your son has only seven days to live."

The troubled Brahmin parents started crying in agony.

"Oh dear Ascetic… what is the reason for that? Is there any way we can save him?"

"My dear friend, I'm afraid I do not have the ability to see the reason for his short lifespan and

also I do not know if there is a way to save him. But I have heard that the God Sakka died and regained his life as God Sakka with a lifespan of thirty six million human-years while listening to Dhamma and worshipping the Supreme Buddha Gauthama. Therefore, I think the Supreme Buddha Gauthama will be able to sort this problem and help you" said the Ascetic.

"But my friend, the Buddha Gauthama does not approve of practicing these austerities, so He might not consider my problem" said the Brahmin.

"Friend, put your pride in your ascetic life aside now!... Think about your son!... You can worry about your ideas later!"

Thereafter, the Brahmin parents took their son to see the Supreme Buddha. First the parents worshipped the Buddha. "May you live long!" blessed the Buddha. Then the parents made the child worship the Buddha. The Supreme Buddha remained silent.

The worried Brahmin parents looked at each other completely baffled. They became very anxious.

"Oh! Please my lord…. Please bless this child wishing him long life as You blessed us" cried the parents.

"Dear Brahmin, this child of yours has only seven days to live. A daemon called 'Awaruddhaka' will come in seven days and kill this child to avenge a grudge started in a previous life. This is the peril this child has ahead of him."

The parents lamented, "Oh…my lord! We raised our little boy with so many plans and so much hope… please my lord…oh….please save our son from this daemon's attack….."

"If so, make a dais at your home. I will ask my disciples to go to your home. For the next seven days they will recite the Noble Dhamma that I have taught for the benefit of all. The merits that accumulate through reciting the Noble Dhamma will protect your child."

Auwaddana Kumaraya

The Brahmin quickly did what the Supreme Buddha requested. On the seventh day the Buddha Himself came to the Brahmin's home along with the Bhikkhus. Because of the infinite powers of the virtues of the Supreme Buddha, the Gods and other celestial beings from all over the universe also attended the Brahmin's home. The daemon Awaruddhaka had only that day to take revenge on the boy. The daemon came to the Brahmin's home and watched from afar. He could not come closer. He was frightened when he saw the Supreme Buddha.

"Oh…no… how can I kill that human child!!! He is near the most exalted Buddha, the majestic teacher of all three worlds. I cannot even go anywhere near him, let alone kill him. Ah! They collected great merits that overpowered my chance to kill that child. Hmm…. it's ok, I will let go of this hatred. It is I who will get into a heap trouble if I try to kill that boy now."

Having thought so, the daemon left for good. He did not come back for the child. On the eighth

day morning, the parents made their son worship the Supreme Buddha.

"Dear son, may you live long!" the Buddha blessed the little boy.

"Oh my lord, for how long will our son live now?" asked the parents.

"Your son will live for hundred and twenty years" replied the most compassionate Buddha.

From that day on, the boy was called 'Ayuwaddana Kumaraya' meaning the boy who gained long life. The whole family took refuge in the Noble Triple Gem, they listened to the Dhamma with great respect and realized it.

Many years passed and the boy grew up. The bhikkhus started talking about what happened when he was a boy. Once he came to see the Buddha and asked him how to gain longevity.

"This truly is a miracle. That noble person had only seven days to live when he met the Buddha as a little boy. Now he has grown up and is living a virtuous life according to Dhamma with a group of five hundred noble men. This shows that there are things that extend one's lifespan."

When the Supreme Buddha heard the bhikkhus' talk, He addressed the bhikkhus thus;

"Dear bhikkhus, when a person worships noble individuals who have eliminated defilements, not only does he live longer, but also his troubles and worries disappear. He will gain four benefits; a long life, a beautiful complexion, comforts and power."

Having said that, the Supreme Buddha recited this stanza as well.

"Abhiwadanaseelissa
      - Niccan waddhapacaino
Cattaro Dhamma waddhanti
      - Ayu, Wanno, Sukhan, Balan"

Auwaddana Kumaraya

The meaning of that stanza is;

For one who is in the habit of constantly honouring and respecting the elders and paying homage to venerable monks, gains for things in life; long life, beauty, happiness and strength.

Now lets learn and remember the meaning of the stanza in a poem like this;

If someone worships with – sincere respect
Noble Ones, Elders who - are wise and righteous
He gains four benefits – when he does it often
Long life, complexion - power and joy abundant

- The end -

Mahamegha English Publications

Sutta Translations
Stories of Sakka, Lord of Gods: Sakka Saṁyutta
Stories of Great Gods: Brahma Saṁyutta
Stories of Heavenly Mansions: Vimānavatthu
Stories of Ghosts: Petavatthu
The Voice of Enlightened Monks: Theragāthā

Dhamma Books
The Wise Shall Realize

Children's Picture Books
The Life of the Buddha for Children
Chaththa Manawaka
Sumana the Novice Monk
Stingy Kosiya of Town Sakkara
Kisagothami
Kali the She-Devil
Ayuwaddana Kumaraya
Sumana the Florist
Sirigutta and Garahadinna
The Banker Anāthapiṇḍika

To order, go to www.mahamevnawa.lk

www.ingramcontent.com/pod-product-compliance
Lightning Source LLC
Chambersburg PA
CBHW041235040426

42444CB00002B/168